"[James] Longenbach's lyric poems hold in them the leaf-lost trees, rising waters, and salt-corroded bricks of a tenuously balanced life. It is hard, sometimes, to differentiate life from loss, love from longing, or Venice, Italy, from the stream-strewn coastal stretches of New Jersey. Everything is connected in the taut, interwoven poems contained in *Forever*." —Camille T. Dungy, *Orion*

"Longenbach knows the difficulty of being in time, of having the experience but missing the meaning. . . . Throughout *Forever*, Longenbach continues to occupy, with effort and imperfection, that strange lyric temporality that is always 'right behind us, waiting to be experienced now.'" —Anthony Domestico, *Commonweal*

"In his poems, James Longenbach not only takes us to a place where the consequence of living is poetry's consequence, but also the consequence of reading is not only to live more fully, but to feel more alive while reading. This is the 'event' of *Forever*, one that allows itself to be repeated in our return to its pages."
 —Peter Filkins, *Salmagundi*

"Magnificent. At once elemental—Freud might say 'oceanic'—in its psychic vista, yet particular as one man's life, loves, and losses, *Forever* is a wrenchingly personal account of memory, sorrow, and profound beauty, rendered in lyric poetry. It is also James Longenbach's finest book, wrought of remarkable paradoxes—to be so precise, so spare, yet to be so inclusive, so elegant—where mortality shadows every erotic or tender gesture. That such existential breadth of vision comes at our moments of deepest crisis is—let me be clear—never a given. But it is, in *Forever*, Longenbach's gift." —David Baker

"In the pages of this tender, immediate, sharp book, you can find something our world has made nearly impossible: language freed of lies that nevertheless consoles. James Longenbach turns his cry outward, as if toward a friend in a future he won't see, surveying childhood and marriage, surface and depth, Europe and America, with a sonic minimalism buoyed as much by the comedy in our affairs as the tragedy of their brevity. I'm certain I'll remember the most beautiful poems in this book for my entire human life."

—Katie Peterson

"The poems in *Forever* wash over you like waves, lift you up and set you down back at the beginning of your life. Some of the people are familiar; the landscape is beautifully strange. You pick up your favorite book and start reading it again, but for the first time. Longenbach's lucid poems echo across decades, bound for poetry's future."

—Rob Schlegel

"The lyric poems of James Longenbach's *Forever* devastate, for they enact with such precision the very problem they pronounce: that the pleasure of the language we read can, like memory, only approach the lives we actually live. Line by line, the poems' likelihood to narrate, repeat, or gorgeously veer describes what it is to love and simultaneously feel oneself inside the grandiosity of time."

—Sally Keith

FOREVER

FOREVER

POEMS

James Longenbach

W. W. NORTON & COMPANY
Celebrating a Century of Independent Publishing

For information about permission to reproduce selections from this book, write to
Permissions, W. W. Norton & Company, Inc., 500 Fifth Avenue, New York, NY 10110

For information about special discounts for bulk purchases, please contact
W. W. Norton Special Sales at specialsales@wwnorton.com or 800-233-4830

Manufacturing by Lakeside Book Company
Production manager: Beth Steidle

Library of Congress Cataloging-in-Publication Data

Names: Longenbach, James, author.
Title: Forever : poems / James Longenbach.
Description: First edition. | New York : W. W. Norton & Company, 2021.
Identifiers: LCCN 2021009362 | ISBN 9780393866537 (hardcover) |
ISBN 9780393866544 (epub)
Subjects: LCGFT: Poetry.
Classification: LCC PS3562.O4967 F67 2021 | DDC 811/.54—dc23
LC record available at https://lccn.loc.gov/2021009362

ISBN 978-1-324-05206-7 pbk.

W. W. Norton & Company, Inc., 500 Fifth Avenue, New York, N.Y. 10110
www.wwnorton.com

W. W. Norton & Company Ltd., 15 Carlisle Street, London W1D 3BS

1 2 3 4 5 6 7 8 9 0

TO JOIE

CONTENTS

I

Two People · 13
Notre-Dame · 16
The Way I Like Best · 18
In the Dolomites · 22
112th Street · 32

II

Thursday · 35
Since February · 36
In the Village · 40
Venice · 46
Via Sacra · 49

III

Barcarolle · 53
School Street · 57
Song of the Sun · 58
This Little Island · 65
Forever · 70

Acknowledgments · 75

I

TWO PEOPLE

Two people at the end of a dock, facing the sea, the sky.
Behind them a party, clink of glasses.
Guests still relevant to their lives
But not essential;
Parents, family friends.

Two people not yet old, but no longer young.
Before them the harbor, they're facing west, they're watching the
    sun go down.
The sky is bright, and then, remarkably, it's dark again.

They've never done this before,
They've done it a thousand times.

The sun goes down,
The stars come out,
Even the lights above the patio are beautiful.

2.

How do you imagine the shape of one lifetime?
A circle, a tangle of lines? He knows
That if he kisses her
She'll kiss him back,
But he waits, they're going to spend their lives together; he knows
   that, too.

Behind them, growing louder, the past:
The one who left, the one who would not go away—

What happens when a wish comes true?
A room by the sea, a bed, a chair.

You're a little sunburnt, a breeze, white curtains billowing,
And as you raise your arms
She lifts the tee shirt from your body.
Perfect gentleness, the perfect glint of pain.

3.

Where will we be in five years, five years after that?
This is a game they play.
Often they play it in a restaurant, Rue de L'Espoir.
A basket of bread, two round glasses of wine. How free they feel!

Five years from now I want us each to have a book.
We'll live in London, maybe Rome.

Five years from that we'll have a baby, what will we name her? She'll
    be a girl.

It all comes true—everything
They ever wished
And more, two girls.

Remember the party behind them, the voices?
They never went away.
But the sound of the sea grew louder.

NOTRE-DAME

High above our heads the forest
Is burning, oaks and chestnuts almost a thousand years old.
Smoke is rising, alarms are ringing,
But down here in the past
We're ignorant, we're unprepared.

This boy lights a candle in a little red cup.
Maybe the girl he loves
No longer loves him.
Look at her, she's standing right beside him; isn't he dumb?

This boy's going to be a father, he's just found out.
Together with his wife
He'll celebrate at Le Trumilou, their favorite bistro, just across the
    Seine.

Viollet-le-Duc is sketching a buttress.
Louis Vierne is playing Bach, the *Toccata and Fugue in D Minor.*
They're embellishers, both of them,
They can't leave the past alone! Doesn't anyone
Hear the sirens, see the black smoke
Billowing against the sky?

The forest is burning. Beneath it
Little flames of hope
Are burning, too.
Hope, desire, longing, fear—

This boy doesn't know he has cancer. This boy
Doesn't realize that, being
Who he is, he asks too much;
The people he loves need less of him.

This boy? He will live forever
In a little house by the sea.

THE WAY I LIKE BEST

Initially the fragments were discovered by Helena,
Mother of the emperor Constantine.
Where precisely, or in what circumstances,
Nobody knows for sure.
Stolen by the Persians in 614,

.

They were recovered intact by Heraclius,
Emperor of the East, in 628.
But because the blood of Jesus had rendered the wood
Imperishable, no matter
How many pieces were removed,

.

The fragments were divided into increasingly smaller fragments,
Each of them, because more easily concealed,
More valuable than the last.
Smuggled out of Jerusalem by two friars,
Entrusted to the Patriarch of Constantinople in 1366,

.

Two such splinters were delivered *nel palmo*,
In the palm of the hand,
To the guardian of the Scuola Grande San Giovanni Evangelista,

One of the six Venetian *scuole* or guilds.
There, in the Oratorio della Croce,

.

You'll find the cross-shaped reliquary in which the splinters,
Arranged to mimic
A cross, are encased in rock crystal.
You won't find the cycle of narrative paintings
Commemorating their acquisition, because in 1806, after dissolving
    the *scuole*,

.

Napoleon removed the paintings from the walls.
Gentile Bellini, Carpaccio, Perugino—
Each depicts the reliquary.
Each depicts a miracle,
Though in Bellini's *Miracle of the Merchant Jacopo de Salis*

.

The miracle is hard to find.
Jacopo, robed in red,
The only person
Kneeling in a sea
Of white-cowled celebrants

•

Carrying the cross to which he prays,
Is completely alone.
His son is dying,
It's the feast of San Marco,
The presentation of the true cross, April 25, 1444—

•

To see the *Miracle of the Merchant Jacopo de Salis* properly,
As for thirty years I did not, remember that in the Scuola
It was hung above your head;
In the Accademia you'll need to kneel.
To see the reliquary of the Scuola Grande San Giovanni Evangelista,

•

Start in the southwest corner of the Campo San Giacomo,
The one with the sycamores you like.
Cross the bridge, turn left, then right, then left again—
The first time I ever saw Venice
I loved you. The second time

·

You loved me, too.
The fifteenth I was sick,
The sixteenth well—
Somewhere, every day, a son gets out of bed.
There are faster ways to get there, simpler ways,

·

But I like this way best.

IN THE DOLOMITES

I.

The afternoon walk, it turns out, may not have been a walk at all.
Nor can I locate in the Dolomites the place
Where we met, though I remember

It with a level of detail I reserve
For things of consequence.
Snow layered in the crevices, white against black. Impossible

Patches of green where grass
Showed through, and more impossible
The gentians, still blooming, yellow against green.

For the color above our heads, heaven, the sky—
I had no word for that.
No one did; remember

This happened a long time ago.
Even if it existed in the world, in your eyes,
Blue did not exist yet in my mind.

2.

I see a rectangular, steeply sloping meadow.
At the top of the meadow a cottage,
And in front of the cottage door

Two women are standing, one with a kerchief on her head.
Children are gathering flowers,
A girl and a boy, the latter of whom is me.

And because the girl has gathered the more prodigious bunch,
I grab it from her; she runs
Up the meadow in tears. To console her

The woman in a kerchief cuts a slice of black bread,
Then slathers it with with jam.
I throw the flowers to the ground, run to the cottage,

And ask to be given bread, too.
In fact I am given some.
The woman cuts the loaf with a long knife.

3.

When I was young I had a beautiful body.
Don't imagine me proud, you had one, too; everybody did.
Just walking down the street or

Looking out the window, sitting on a train,
Was like staring
Into the sun. Modesty

Made nothing happen
Since the parts
Were more enticing than the whole.

I read a lot of books. I drove
Long distances with the windows down. Who were
The ones with golden eyes and sunlit hair

Who lounged all day beside the river clearly
Doing something important
Though it looked like nothing at all?

4.

At twelve I returned to Bolzano for the first time.
Always I'd longed for the meadows
Of my childhood, where I'd escaped from my father even

When I could barely walk. But when I returned,
Something else excited me greatly:
A thirteen-year-old girl, the daughter of my hosts, who last I'd seen
     at four.

Immediately I fell in love—
My first infatuation,
Though I said nothing to anyone.

After a few days, the girl returned to school, as soon I did, too.
But in the interim I spent my afternoons
Wandering in the meadows, the mountains

Rising, as they always had, abruptly from my feet.
My fantasies were not directed at the future,
But rather sought to improve the past.

5.

Two children walking through the meadow where they were born.
Born there like animals, suckled by a she-wolf
Together in one bed, one bower.

When one of them smiled, they both smiled.
When one of them frowned,
Together they frowned, furrowed their brows, so serious, so stern!

Then together they laughed.
Together they ate, together they slept,
Their legs tangled up together,

Legs brown from the sun.
Together they forgot the past, they invented
The future, the bower, the bed—

Then it was morning. One of us got in the car,
One of us stood at the door
And waved good-bye.

6.

Knowledge, as the ancients remind us,
Is conventional; not in the sense of
Arbitrary, but because it depends

On qualities we cannot observe.
Atom, from *atomos*, meaning indivisible.
So if the atoms of water

Are slippery and smooth,
The atoms of salt are pointed,
While the atoms of red things quiver like flame.

On the color blue Democritus is silent.
So is Homer, who calls the sea
Oinops, wine-dark, or, more literally, wine-looking.

The hides of oxen, to our eyes brown or black,
Also he calls *oinops*. The sky
He calls *starry, broad, iron,* or *copper.*

I'm looking at a boy and a girl, no longer boy and girl.
Together they have not only the future,
They have a past. She's reading

Letters he's written; he's leaning his head against her neck,
He's curling his arm behind her slender waist,
His fingers emerging, from my viewpoint,

Just below her breast.
Gently they're touching her breast.
Remember how that felt?

Behind them a garden, the meeting, the pursuit.
Is the shrubbery tended or overgrown, the columbines
Luxurious because they're trimmed?

Yellow her bodice, green the trees.
Are the branches closing off the sky, or parting
To reveal it, a smudge of blue?

8.

At this point in the narrative
I remember very little; whole years fall away.
Time, if you'll permit me the expression, stood still.

Yes, there were children of our own, we moved to Treviso.
Then it was morning.
You were standing at the door.

Why won't you come with me,
Why must I go alone,
Asked the first person ever to die.

When finally I admitted, to my shame, *this is the worst thing*
That's ever happened to me,
What had happened was almost nothing.

But I'd never seen it before, I had no
Word to describe it,
Though it was everywhere.

9.

The windows were open, the ledges
Of the balcony broad: the sweep of the canal
And the flutter of the white curtains were an invitation to

—I couldn't have said what. A reef, over which had broken,
Through long ages, the billows of an angry sea?
When the fog rising from the intervening

Plains and lagoons had lifted,
There they were: towers
And ramparts, battlements, pinnacles, the deepest

Of deep reds, the blackest black
Against a cobalt sky.
Mountains, stars, calves, serpents, fever,

War, fame, vice, adultery—these are among the things
That cannot take the place
Of heaven, though people have tried.

10.

In my first life, my body was fresh, unaccustomed to itself.
I learned to read, to make love.
Maybe it was like this for you, too. In my second

I was asked to be older; when I advertised
My interests they proved
Interesting to other people. What interested me?

The trees grew taller, the houses stayed the same.
And when I was summoned again
I had to count out loud—

Was this the fourth time, the fifth?
A stranger remembered me;
You lived here, he said, a long time ago. The trees

Had grown taller, the children were more beautiful than ever
Or had they always been so,
Smiling at one another, staring at the sky?

If only once, if ever you have the chance,
You should climb a volcano.
The hermitage at base camp, the glasses of brandy—
That's the past.
Who wants to think about the past?

You want to push forward, climb higher, while all around you,
Inches beneath your feet,
Earth is seething, a river of liquid rock.

Will you make it to the summit—
The flying slag, the potholes
Red as an open wound?
Of course you will, it's easy; everybody does.

So little behind you,
So much ahead—

Once, walking up Broadway
Late at night,
Both of us a little drunk, flurries in the air, Christmas trees
Lining the sidewalk, block after block—

At every corner
You kissed me.
Then the light would change.

II

THURSDAY

Because the most difficult part about making something, also the
    best,
Is existing in the middle,
Sustaining an act of radical imagination,
I simmered a broth: onion, lemon, a big handful of mint.

The phone rang. So with my left
Hand I answered it,
Sautéing the rice, then adding the broth
Slowly, one ladle at a time, with my right—*hello?*—

The miracle, it's easy to miss, is the moment when the husks
    dissolve,
Each grain releasing its tiny explosion of starch.

If you take it off the heat just then, let it sit
While you shave the parmesan into paper-thin curls,
It will be perfectly creamy,
But will still have a bite.

There will be dishes to do,
The moon will rise,
And everyone you love will be safe.

SINCE FEBRUARY

Russ

Your mother is driving you out of Texas,
She's heading east on Route 10,
The top is down, the wind is blowing through her hair.

Chattanooga? That was hours ago.
Martinsburg, Harrisburg—
You've never seen the ocean, you could see the ocean—

First stop: the Vermeers
At the Metropolitan, gallery 899.
Second, Maria Callas, seats in the parterre.

Mark

Eyebrows raised as you uncorked the cognac, dishes cleared,
The children screaming in the living room—
Grow old along with me.

Eight years later resting on a bench
In the Piazza Santo Spirito—
Getting old is not for sissies.

You by the window overlooking the park at Ninety-First Street,
Unable to walk
There, looking to read.

Wendy

Addio, per sempre addio, per sempre,
Sings Elisabetta to Don Carlo at the end of act five;
Per sempre, sings the don. Inevitably

This story ends, we had a train to make.
Feet dangling beneath you,
One of us hoisting you by your left arm, another by your right,

You flew down the Via Venti Settembre
While the rest of us ran.
Your beaming face.

Bianca

Although we're standing on the icy wing of an airplane
In the middle of the Hudson River,
Nobody dies today.

Although the ruins of Palmyra have been ruined again,
Ruins I saw first in *Life* magazine,
I was a boy, summer of '66,

Nobody dies today. All we did
Was leave the door open.
And you disappeared.

Sandy

After the torchlight red on sweaty faces,
The lectures and the arguments,
The students listening politely in rows—

You with a bottle of chardonnay and a package of Ritz crackers
Pinched from the reception.
Meet you in my room!

And a thousand years before that: you
At the Academy, letting me sit
In Edith Wharton's chair.

Maureen

I'm wearing the cardigan you sent me, the blue one;
I saved the box in which it came.
I'm walking across the park, I'm sitting

In brilliant sunshine on the steps of the museum, a taxi pulls up—
Everybody's alive.
Where is he exactly,

You asked, unable to imagine
A life alone.
Where are you now?

Russ

A singer in the moment before he opens his mouth,
Said Charles Anthony, who stood on the Met stage 2,928 times,
Is the loneliest person in the world.

Love of words, mouths shaping words, your taste, equally exquisite,
For the vulgar—I dreamt
About a department meeting: there, primly

At a little desk, you were waiting.
What are you doing here?
Where else, you answered, *would I be?*

IN THE VILLAGE

Shortly before I died,
Or possibly after,
I moved to a small village by the sea.

You'll recognize it, as did I, because I've written
About this village before.
The rocky sliver of land, the little houses where the fishermen once
    lived—

We had everything we needed: a couple of rooms
Overlooking the harbor,
A small collection of books,
Paperbacks, the pages
Brittle with age.

How, if I'd never seen
The village, had I pictured it so accurately?
How did I know we'd be happy there,
Happier than ever before?

The books reminded me of what,
In our youth,
We called literature.

2.

The sentences I've just written
Took it out of me.
I searched for the words,
And I resisted them as soon as I put them down.

Now, listening to them again, what I hear
Is not so much nostalgia
As a love of beginning. A wish

Not to be removed
From time but
Always to be immersed in it.
The boats come in, the boats go out—

3.

After a routine ultrasound revealed a fifteen-centimeter mass, my left kidney was removed robotically on February 12. Fifteen months later, nodules were discovered in my lungs and peritoneum. Two subsequent rounds of therapy failed to impede their growth, so I enrolled in a trial, a treatment not yet FDA approved.

I walked down High Street to the harbor, though when I say *walked* I mean imagined; I hadn't been there yet.

4.

Of ghosts pursued, forgotten, sought anew—
Everywhere I go
The trees are full of them.

From trees come books, that, when they open,
Lead you to expect a person
On the other side:

One hand having pulled
The doorknob
Toward him, the other

Held out, open,
Beckoning
You forward—

The Branch Will Not Break.

A Cold Spring.

Leaflets.

The Lost World.

The Moving Target.

Nightmare Begins Responsibility.

Rivers and Mountains.

The Story of Our Lives.

Untitled Subjects.

Water Street.

6.

Ash-blond, tall, a sweater
Knotted by its sleeves around his neck,
A boy is leaning on a bicycle. Deftly when she reaches him

A girl slips to the grass, one hand straightening her skirt,
The other tugging at the boy,
Who remains standing, to sit beside her.

Their heads are close
Enough to be touching;
Their lips are still—

A book is the future.
You dream
Of reading it, and once you've finished, it's a miracle, you know the
    past.

The sky fills with stars. The sun
Climbs every morning
Over Watch Hill, dropping behind the harbor at dusk.

Water Street runs past
Church and Wall,
Harmony and School,
Until it crosses Omega, by the sea.

VENICE

Before the pedestrian bridges had railings, before most people knew how to swim, the water entrance would have been the Hotel Daniele's fulcrum, the hub of its staff's solicitations. *The beginning of everything was in seeing the gondola-beak come actually inside the door at the Daniele*: for centuries it's been impossible to see Venice except through the images of Canaletto and Turner, the sentences of Shakespeare and Byron, but the teen-aged John Ruskin nonetheless experienced the beginning of everything—not just a discovery of a lifelong passion for Venice but the discovery of eros itself.

.

Nobody has been there before. Every time you walk from a typically mid-century train station onto the water—the vaporetti unloading their cargo of tourists, the dome of San Simeone Piccolo hovering on the other side, improbably larger than the portico beneath it—you do so for the first time. Even when you know the city well enough to navigate alone, getting lost is easy, but so is being found—look where I am! Walk out to the Ognissanti at nine o'clock at night, the water black and still, look down toward San Nicolò dei Mendicoli, founded in the seventh century, built over the next millennium, and you might be anyone living in the year 2020 or 1520.

.

I grew up in New Jersey, not far from New York, not far from the Jersey shore. Though New Jersey has more coastline per square mile than Alaska or Hawaii, water seemed to me exotic. Cranford, the town next door, where my father taught art at the high school, is bisected by the meandering Rahway River, and after Hurricane Alma in the summer of '66, the river's twists and turns were obliterated, the houses along its banks submerged in a vast sheet of shimmering water.

•

Venice, as everyone knows, is sinking. Its buildings settle a little deeper, year after year, into the layer of silt on which they were made. At the same time, the water is rising, transgressing the layers of impervious Istrian stone laid on a foundation of innumerable tree trunks. The lagoon is the crux of Venetian hegemony: in what other medieval city does the center of government, the home of its ruler, stand completely unprotected, meters from the sea, flaunting its delicate opulence? But as the level of the lagoon rises, salt water wicks into the courses of brick laid above the stone. The MOSE project, an expensive plan to install mobile barriers at the mouths of the lagoon, has been debated for decades, and meanwhile the atrium of San Marco floods over half the days of the year.

•

Like anyone, I could slip in the bathtub. Looking at myself in the mirror, I was forced to rethink everything: returning to Venice bolstered my relationship to contingency, though I can't evade the suspicion that New Jersey might have suited me just as well.

•

Start in the northwest corner of the Campo San Giacomo, behind the garden with its stand of sycamores. Take a right on the first bridge crossing the canal, turn sharply to the left, as quickly you must, then take another right on the Calle del Tentor. If you keep walking straight, or as straight as you can, you'll come to the Campo Santa Maria Mater Domini, unremarkable except for the row of elegant Gothic windows gracing the dilapidated fourteenth-century Palazzetto Viaro on its west side. Beneath the central window is a low relief of the Venetian lion, symbol of the Republic, that was half scratched out by Napoleon's soldiers in 1797, when after a thousand years of independence the Republic welcomed an outsider.

VIA SACRA

Imagine the most beautiful girl in the world is walking in front of
    you.
She's entering the ruins of western civilization,
The wind is swirling her skirt
Around her thighs.

You want to follow. But you know
She wants to be alone
With western civilization; she's holding a map.

Little boy, one day your hand will hover above the spinning record
As you drop
The stylus on the Berg quartet.

You will retain this memory, return to it,
Because she'll write it down.

III

BARCAROLLE

Empedocles on Etna is a poem
By the Victorian poet Matthew Arnold.
Readily I'll concede that poetry is a criticism of life (his phrase)
About as much as red-hot iron
Is a criticism of fire,

*

But we're in Sicily.
The gods are still with us.
The sun has warmed the rocks
On which we're lounging, eating goat cheese, drinking new wine.
You're hardly wearing any clothes.

*

Nobody's wearing clothes!
Neither is anyone
Worried about sunlight.
This is before Jesus, before Socrates,
Before the double onslaught of guilt and rationality

*

Doomed us (I'm paraphrasing Nietzsche) to believe
In the rectification of the world

Through knowledge—to live
Within the limited circle of soluble problems,
Where we may cheerfully say to life

.

I want you! You're worth knowing!
Empedocles is having a bad day.
Once, he was a god;
Smart, good-looking, too.
You understand how anyone might feel that way

.

Just being where we are, tasting things, just breathing the air.
Above us, Etna's cone
Emits its languorous white plume.
Miracles? *Mistrust them*, says Empedocles.
Mind is a spell that governs

.

Heaven and earth.
Is it so small a thing
To have enjoyed the sun,
To have lived lightly in the spring,
To have loved, to have thought, to have done?

•

Obvious as the answer to this question may be, convincing, too,
Empedocles climbs beyond the ashen trees,
The potholes red as an open wound,
And steps into a cloud.
A poem of passive suffering, said Arnold,

•

Could have no place in his collected poems.
No place. His greatest poem! Whose suffering
Isn't passive? What else
Could suffering be?
One night in Venice

•

I couldn't sleep; I heard the bells
Of San Giacomo ring four times, then five.
I heard the mutter of a boat, two voices, a woman's and a man's,
Then somehow rising
Between them, as from the water itself,

•

The Chopin *Barcarolle*.
Who could they have been?
Why were they playing
Chopin in their little boat,
Playing it softly, just for me? Remember

.

When we lived like forest creatures,
You and I, when all
We left behind were footsteps
Crushed in the wet grass?
When I opened my eyes

.

Sun-stirred water played
Across the ceiling;
You were asleep.
It felt like being
In the present, being alive.

SCHOOL STREET

The person I once was found himself
In the present, which was the only place he could be.
The dog that yesterday had barked
At his empty dish barked again.
The stars were still shining,
Though the brilliance of the sun obscured them so completely
You'd believe they'd disappeared.
Time to walk to the paddock.
Will the roses be blooming? Will Penny be there, too?
Selfishly we planted cornflowers, delphiniums,
A different bed for every shade.
From behind the wisteria came children, then grandchildren—
The girls wore smocked dresses, dresses my mother
Had made, the boys had floppy hair.
The things we made
Ourselves seemed permanent,
But like the stars invisible, even the things
We made from words. Downstairs
The kitchen, the living room, everything in place:
The bed could fold up in the wall.
But upstairs a ladder where each evening, one by one,
We'd climb into the crow's nest
To rehearse the stars. Hold the railing! Don't fall!
How did we afford this house?
Why, if it exists
In the present,
Am I speaking in the past?

SONG OF THE SUN

I.

Two children side by side
In the cathedral at twilight, knowing
They'd missed the train.
And once, just
Before dawn, they stumbled
Down an alley, it was Christmas,
To a courtyard strung with tiny yellow lights.
They learned to read,
To make love. The fields
Grew taller than their foreheads,
And the trees sent taproots
Deep into the ground.

2.

What happened next
Had never happened before
Though it would happen again.
From her body came forth another body not
More beautiful but beautiful
In a different way.
Immediately
There were people who helped them care for this body,
Feed it, clothe it,
But when this happened
Again, it had never
Happened before.

3.

Song of the First First Child

In the middle of a steep staircase
I fell asleep I didn't know
Whether to look forward
Or back each step
Looked dangerous to me
You called this being born I call it
Making a sandwich
Taking the bus if
You could understand me
I would tell you
Everything I'd show you
Sunlight on my golden hair

4.

Song of the Second First Child

Before I could walk I
Walked through snow a forest
Shagged with ice who's there
Said the bird I could not
Say I could say
Only what I'd heard before I said
It differently there was
A little girl she could not
Speak she spoke
The pine trees
Shagged with ice she said
You're beautiful

5.

To imagine you've changed is to preserve
The person you once were.
Alternatively, to recognize you've
Never changed, that now you
See yourself as then you
Didn't, couldn't,
Even if you'd tried,
Is to feel
Viscerally a part
Of time, to collaborate
In the project of becoming, always
To have begun.

6.

What happens next takes
Seconds, it takes a thousand years.
A dog barks once,
A cricket chirps, the children
Lift their heads to breathe in fields, a flag
Snapping in the wind, the sun
A daub of Tintoretto's
Crimson sliding into the Great Salt Pond—let's
Count together,
Kathryn, Alice, Marc,
Jillian, Owen, Adam, everybody,
Five, four, three, two—

7.

Song of the Sun

No matter where
You are no
Matter where I
Go if you are
Speaking
To me I have
Said this
Before I say
It now I will be
Listening
To you
Speak

THIS LITTLE ISLAND

I.

Outside the room where you have lived a long time
Are other rooms, another building, just like yours.

Each night a ship sails past, wider than the building, taller than the
    highest church.
And though the passengers come to visit the city,
No one in the city ever boards the ship. Would you?

Each night this spectacle is seen by you.
The street surveyed,
The air inhaled.

Grapes from the west,
Cinnamon from the east—

If I've employed too liberally the passive voice,
Remember it's the thoughts, the feelings
That matter here,
Not the one who feels them.

2.

Shall we walk to the market?
You could walk there blind, like Gloucester, smelling your way.

Shall we stop for coffee? Which café?
The one that's commandeered by women, delicate cups?
Or the one where men preside, baristas in tuxedos, the coffee rich
    enough for rainy days?

A window, the desk, a lamp and a chair—
You've liked the room, you like to rearrange it for winter,
Put things back for spring.

But you've been young for a long time,
An embarrassingly long time.
Look what you wrote!
Remember how much, despite
Your ridiculous behavior, you've been loved.

3.

The city never changes, it's never the same.
Sometimes the inhabitants restore a building, patch it up,
But in a generation they're dissatisfied, they try again,
Expose the old parts so you see them
Plainly, ruined or not.

Who schooled you?
What made you scared of change?

Vividly you remember a child's body; likewise you remember a
    man's.
You woke up one morning,
There you were, a stinking adult.

What happened between? What will it be like,
You've seen the images, to watch your body spoiling
From the inside out, your lungs, your neck,
The muscles in your face—

Look out the window,
Choose a single brick.
Once, a long time ago, the city was old.

4.

Clouds desire the sky, the sky the sun. The wave
Desires the land it's eroding,
Repeating the same question, day after day—
Am I allowed to ask for what I want?

And every day the land responds
Of course you're allowed.
You're allowed to be angry,
You're allowed to curse the God who put you here.

I've buried many people, old people, young people.
I've buried children while their parents wept beside the grave.

But I've also seen miracles.
Remember when they told you
You might die? You didn't, you're alive.
And every month since then, every second is a miracle.

What happens next you cannot know.
Is it better or worse to live a long time?
Really the words better and worse do not obtain.

And when the land stops speaking
The wave flows out to sea.

5.

Close your eyes, unclench your hands.
Relax each muscle in your body, first your forehead, then your neck,
Your chest, your arms, how young you are, you've never
Done this before, you've done it a thousand times—

Outside, the walls of San Trovaso are streaked with gold.
Boats are knocking against the Giudecca.
If you stand on tiptoes you can see, above the chimney pots, its
    glistening rim.

Look at all the people, look at their dogs! They're nothing like you,
And they're here.
Who brought you here, who made the bed?

That gasp of pleasure when you entered the room,
First touched the walls,
Whose was it, if it wasn't yours?

FOREVER

Once, in a room no bigger than the bed,
I made love with a girl.

.

Have you ever made love with a girl?
Once I hadn't, then I had.

.

A girl was looking up at me,
She was lying on the grass.

.

Once, after a terrible fight, I made love with a girl.
We were children again.

.

Once, eating ice cream,
I smelled her body on my hands.

.

The first time I made love with a girl I was scared;
I thought I would hurt her.

•

Once in Italy and on the same day,
Once in France.

•

Remember that week in the cabin?
The time in front of the fire, when everyone else was asleep?

•

Once, we made love to make a baby.
Once, a baby was sleeping on the bed.

•

I walked across the park.
A girl pulled her jeans off slowly.

•

Once, making love with a girl,
I thought I was someone else.

•

I was a boy forever.
She pushed me down on the bed.

•

What did we do afterward?
What had I done before?

•

Once, without my noticing, the world turned once,
Then twice, then disappeared.

•

Turned twice, and everything
Was different, everything was the same.

•

Nobody lives forever.
I love you. I love you, too.

.

Once, in a world no bigger than a bed,
You said we'd be lovers forever.

.

That was the first time.
The second was by the sea.

ACKNOWLEDGMENTS

My gratitude to the editors of the following magazines, in which these poems originally appeared:

The Adroit Journal: "Two People"
The American Poetry Review: "In the Village"
The American Scholar: "School Street," "Notre-Dame," "Venice"
The New Yorker: "112th Street"
The Paris Review: "Forever"
Poem-a-Day: "Thursday"
Poetry: "Barcarolle," "This Little Island"
Raritan: "Since February"
Seneca Review: "Song of the Sun"
The Threepenny Review: "In the Dolomites"
The Yale Review: "The Way I Like Best"

"In the Dolomites" is indebted to Sigmund Freud's notion of "screen memories," to W. E. Gladstone's *Studies on Homer*, and to Matthew Von Unwerth's *Freud's Requiem*, as "In the Village" is to J.-B. Pontalis's *Windows* and "Venice" is to John Ruskin's *Praeterita*. "In the Village" was reprinted in *Poetry Daily* at poems.com and also in *The Best American Poetry 2021*, edited by Tracy K. Smith and David Lehman.